Frenem' for Life

CHEETAHS AND ANATOLIAN SHEPHERD DOGS

BY JOHN E. BECKER, Ph.D.

Foreword by Jack Hanna

COLUMBUS
ZOO
AND AQUARIUM

This publication has been made possible through the generous funding of the Frances J. Coultrap Endowment at the Columbus Zoo and Aquarium.

Front cover photo © 2009 Peters Photography
Back cover photos © 2009 Columbus Zoo and Aquarium

Publisher's Cataloging-In-Publication Data
(Prepared by The Donohue Group, Inc.)
Becker, John E., 1942-
    Frenemies for life : cheetahs and Anatolian shepherd dogs / by John E. Becker.
    p. : ill. ; cm.
    Summary: Describes a special program initiated by the Cheetah Conservation Fund
that saves cheetahs from extinction by using Anatolian shepherd dogs to guard farmers'
flocks. Also highlights the Paws and Claws program of the Columbus Zoo, which takes
cheetahs and dogs into schools to teach people about the plight of the cheetah.
    Includes bibliographical references.
    Interest age level: 10 and up.

    ISBN: 978-0-9841554-0-8 (hardcover)
    ISBN: 978-0-9841554-1-5 (pbk.)

1. Cheetah–Africa, Southern–Juvenile literature. 2. Anatolian shepherd dog–Africa,
Southern–Juvenile literature. 3. Livestock–Losses–Africa, Southern–Juvenile literature.
4. Wildlife conservation–Africa, Southern–Juvenile literature. 5. Cheetah Conservation
Fund–Juvenile literature. 6. Columbus Zoo–Juvenile literature. 7. Cheetah–Africa,
Southern. 8. Anatolian shepherd dog–Africa, Southern. 9. Livestock–Losses–Africa,
Southern. 10. Wildlife conservation–Africa, Southern. 11. Cheetah Conservation Fund.
12. Columbus Zoo. I. Title.
QL706.2 .B43 2010
599.759/0968

Published by Columbus
Zoological Park Association
9990 Riverside Drive
Delaware, OH 43065
www.columbuszoo.org

Produced for the Columbus
Zoological Park Association by
School Street Media
info@schoolstreetmedia.com
www.schoolstreetmedia.com

Printed in the United States of America

2 4 6 8 10 9 7 5 3 1

Dedicated to the memories of
Columbus Zoo Director, Jeff Swanagan,
whose visionary leadership of the zoo
included the concept for this book
and to Heather Pick, who as a news anchor
at WBNS-10TV in Columbus, Ohio, was a
strong advocate of the Columbus Zoo and
a champion of wildlife conservation

Contents

JACK HANNA

Foreword

Alert eyes, a striking spotted coat, extraordinary running speed, and the ability to turn on a dime—the cheetah is a fascinating cat! This animal has been revered for ages, and it deserves a place on Earth forever, despite human interference. Unfortunately these cats are facing many challenges in their African homeland and are now listed as an endangered species.

Frenemies for Life, by Dr. John Becker, highlights "everything cheetah" by discussing such topics as prehistoric cheetahs, cheetahs trained by the ancient Egyptians for hunting purposes, the status of cheetahs today, and ultimately, conservation efforts.

Believe it or not, animal conservation is a relatively new idea. Less than a hundred years ago, people still killed wildlife for food, sport, medicinal uses, and other reasons. Scientists began to realize that many of our Earth's animals were vanishing—and we had to do something about it! Thus, "wildlife conservation" was born.

At the Columbus Zoo, the staff is promoting conservation on a daily basis. We felt that the work of the Cheetah Conservation Fund in Namibia was so valuable, we wanted to spread the word here in the U.S. *Frenemies for Life* outlines a new conservation outreach program at the zoo in which two young Anatolian shepherd dogs were raised side-by-side with young cheetahs. So, these "enemies" have become quite good friends!

Creating awareness of the cheetah's survival challenges is crucial in raising funds for cheetah conservation. Inspiration, too, is part of the overall picture. When the zoo presents its program featuring this very compelling story—along with help from the young cheetahs and dogs—people actually see these amazing animals up close and personal. And most are definitely inspired to do more for conservation!

—*Jack Hanna*
Director Emeritus of the Columbus Zoo and Aquarium

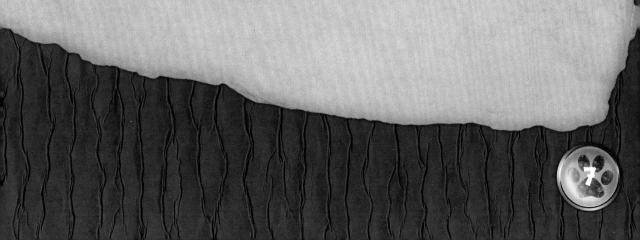

From Natural Enemies to Best of Friends

You've probably heard the saying "they fight like cats and dogs" about people who don't get along with each other. It's easy to see where that saying comes from when you watch a stray cat encounter a dog going down the sidewalk: The cat hisses, the dog barks, and both animals are ready to either attack or run (known as the "fight or flight" response to fear). Are cats and dogs natural enemies? You bet.

Every so often, enemies—sometimes even old enemies—discover they have a common goal and put aside their differences to become friends. When that happens, the word people use to describe that new relationship is "frenemies." This book is about a special program that features some natural enemies who have become great friends—all to share a message about another program, half a world away, where some big dogs are helping some wild cats survive. Why are these cats in danger and how can dogs help them? Let's find out.

The Cheetah Story

All big cats are amazing, but the cheetah stands out as different. One look at the black "tear marks" on its face and the large golden-amber eyes tells you that this is one of the most beautiful animals on Earth. And the "tear marks" are there for a purpose. The marks run from the inside of its eyes down its face, ending at the corners of the cat's mouth. These marks help tone down the sunlight so the cheetah can spot its prey, even at long distances.

TEAR MARKS

Dark "tear marks" help a cheetah see better in bright sunlight. That's the same reason football or baseball players puts black smudges under their eyes!

The cheetah is different in other ways, too. No cat—or any land animal—is faster. The cheetah can go from 0 to 65 miles per hour in about 3 seconds. Even race cars can't do that! This cat can speed at 70 to

FASTEST CAT

75 miles per hour for about 1,500 feet before it runs out of energy and has to rest, making it the sprinter of the cat species. Its extra-large heart and lungs, long tail used as a rudder, and semi-retractable claws that dig in all help the cheetah achieve its speed and agility. Fast as it may be, the cheetah can't climb trees, making it vulnerable to attacks by other big cats.

You might be surprised to learn that lions, leopards, and other big cats can roar, but they cannot purr. Conversely, the cheetah can purr, both as it breathes in and as it breathes out—but it can't roar.

Cheetahs are unique and fragile in so many ways. It's important to learn as much about them as we can, because if we don't find a way to help them, these elegant, swift, awesome animals could be gone within our lifetime.

Cheetahs of the Past

Cheetah-type wild cats have been around for a long time, and in prehistoric times they lived practically all over the world. Their oldest ancestors appeared in North America about 4 million years ago during a time in Earth's history known as the Pliocene period (approximately 5.2 million to 1.6 million years ago). Those ancestors migrated from North America over land and ice bridges into Asia, then Europe, and finally Africa. Fossilized remains of North American cheetahs (*Miracinonyx*) have been uncovered in several locations across the United States. Those ancient cheetahs were very similar to modern cheetahs, except they were much larger; *Miracinonyx* was almost twice the size of today's cheetah. North American cheetahs appear to have been built for speed like their modern-day relatives.

modern cheetah   *Miracinonyx*

ENDANGERED

Name: Cheetah (*Acinonyx jubatus*)
Type: Mammal
Diet: Carnivore
Average lifespan in the wild: 10 to 12 years
Length (not including tail): 3.5 to 4.5 feet (1.1 to 1.4 m)
Weight: 75 to 145 pounds (35 to 65 kg)
Protection status: Endangered

Like many other large mammals of that era, *Miracinonyx* became extinct between 10,000 to 20,000 years ago. Old World cheetahs—our modern cheetahs—still survive today, but they are also in danger of disappearing.

As human populations increased through the ages, cheetah populations declined, gradually disappearing from one part of the world after another. Long ago, cheetahs disappeared from Europe, but some managed to survive in Asia until the twentieth century. Today, almost all wild cheetahs are found in Africa, scattered about in smaller and smaller areas. The one exception is Iran in the Middle East, where fewer than 100 cheetahs live today.

"Hunting Leopards"

People have admired cheetahs and their great speed throughout history. More than 4,000 years ago, the ancient Egyptians became the first people to tame cheetahs as hunting companions for pharaohs, or rulers. The cheetahs were trained like hunting dogs are trained today. But pharaohs also displayed cheetahs as symbols of the rulers' power. Later, rulers in Asia, Europe, and India also used cheetahs as "hunting leopards" and as guardians of their thrones. It must have been quite an impressive sight to enter the royal court and see cheetahs lying on either side of the king's throne. This practice became so popular that many cheetahs were taken from their natural habitats, causing their populations in the wild to become depleted.

Stealthy and sharp-eyed, the cheetah has more than speed to help it catch prey. But this wild cat has some serious disadvantages, too.

Scaredy Cats
and Bullies

From the mighty Amur tigers to the tiny black-footed cats of southern Africa, all the wild cats on Earth today are truly fearless creatures—except one. Despite its size, speed, and skill as a hunter, the cheetah is the "scaredy cat" of the feline family.

Cheetahs have different personalities from other wild cats. If you've ever spent much time around domestic cats, you know that each one has its own personality: serious, shy, goofy, or even hostile. Cheetahs aren't as large as lions and other large predators, and they are not as strong as most other big cats, either. As a result, cheetahs have developed skittish personalities, so they run in the face of danger and avoid conflicts whenever they can. Cheetahs are fortunate to survive at all in the dangerous neighborhoods where they live.

Speed is undoubtedly the cheetahs' best advantage, but speed alone doesn't always help them get a good meal. Since cheetahs are capable of running 70 to 75 miles per hour, you'd think they could catch almost everything they chase, but that's not the case. Scientists tell us that cheetahs are successful only about half the time when they pursue a prey animal. Even when they do make a kill, cheetahs often expend so much energy that they must rest before devouring their catch. That's when the local bullies, other predators like lions, leopards, jackals, hyenas, and even vultures, come along and steal the cheetahs' hard-won meals. When cheetahs lose out to one of those other predators, they have no choice but to start all over and begin stalking another meal.

MANTLE

Cheetah Cubs' Cool Camouflage

Just about everyone knows what an adult cheetah looks like, but many people are surprised when they see a cheetah cub with its thick yellowish-gray mane, or mantle, running down the length of its back. Why does a cheetah cub have a mane? Scientists believe that the furry mane serves as camouflage, allowing the young animal to blend into its surroundings and hide from predators. The mane also gives a cheetah cub the appearance of an extremely aggressive African predator known as a ratel, or honey badger. Ratels are so aggressive that even much larger predators will usually leave them—and the look-alike cheetah cubs—alone.

A Brotherhood of Cheetahs

In the world of wild cats, the lion stands out as the most social cat of all. Lions live in groups of up to 40 individuals, known as prides. Almost all other wild cat species are solitary, meaning the males and females only get together during mating season. Then the males go off on their own, and the females live alone until they give birth to a litter of cubs. After the cubs become old enough to hunt on their own, the mother goes back to being a loner, until mating season comes along again.

The only other wild cats that live in groups beyond childhood are male cheetahs. When male cheetahs leave their mothers, they often continue to hang out with their brothers as hunting partners. These male "coalitions" work out well for the cheetahs, especially when they have to compete with lions, leopards, hyenas, and other predators for their meals. By working cooperatively, male cheetahs can survive in areas where they might otherwise perish if they hunted alone.

BROTHERHOOD

Cheetahs in Danger

It has been estimated that there were as many as 100,000 cheetahs in the world in the early 1900s. Today only 10,000 to 12,500 cheetahs survive. The largest cheetah population is found in Namibia in southern Africa, where an estimated 3,000 free-ranging cheetahs live today. But even in Namibia, there is no safety in numbers for the cheetahs.

Namibia once had a much larger population of cheetahs. Then, in the 1980s, the cheetah population was cut in half, because Namibia suffered a series of devastating droughts. The prey animals that cheetahs normally hunted died off. Also, farmers killed cheetahs and other wild animals to eliminate competition for grazing areas where their live-stock fed. By the beginning of 1990, fewer than 2,500 cheetahs survived in Namibia, and it is now the most endangered cat in Africa.

More than 90 percent of Namibia's cheetahs live on land that has become farms or grazing land. Hungry cheetahs will go after the goats and sheep, because other sources of food are scarce and the farm animals are easy prey.

EASY PREY

Namibian farmers see cheetahs as a threat to their own survival, so they kill cheetahs to protect their herds. And the law is behind the farmers. Even though cheetahs are a protected species in Namibia, people may legally kill cheetahs if they pose a threat to livestock or human life.

Even when they can avoid conflicts with people, cheetahs have difficulty surviving. Few cheetahs born in the wild survive to become adults. Cheetah cubs, usually three to a litter, are especially at risk of being attacked by predators, especially lions. Cheetah mothers' weak jaws and small teeth make it virtually impossible for them to fight off larger predators to protect their young. The cheetahs that survive their first 18 months still face huge challenges after they leave their mothers' protective care.

Despite all of the factors working against the cheetahs, some hopeful signs have appeared over the past decade due to the efforts of conservation organizations.

Dogs: The Cheetah's New Best Friend

It is early morning in Namibia in southern Africa. A herd of goats grazes peacefully as rays of sunlight slowly move across the grassy plain. The only sound is the soft tinkling of tiny bells the goats wear around their necks.

A short distance away, hidden in the tall grass, a figure waits quietly. The large cheetah has crept within a few yards of the herd.

As the goats continue to nibble on the grass, the cheetah crouches low, tensing its muscles. Its steady gaze is fixed on one of the small goats grazing apart from the others.

Then the cheetah explodes from the grass in a blur of black and yellow.

Suddenly, a large, powerful dog comes from nowhere, barking and snarling, his teeth bared, racing straight at the wild cat. The cheetah stops abruptly, frightened by the animal charging at it, whirls around, and speeds out of harm's way.

Of course, the cheetah didn't see the dog as its friend. But this guard dog is the best friend the cheetah could have—because it has probably saved the cheetah's life.

The Livestock Guarding Dog Program

The Cheetah Conservation Fund (CFF) was founded in 1990 by Dr. Laurie Marker to help keep cheetahs from disappearing from their natural habitats. CCF also conducts research across the cheetah's range to help determine the biological status of cheetahs and their ecology. Before 1990, cheetahs in Namibia were being killed at a rate of about 800 to 900 per year, until only about 3,000 cheetahs remained.

Dr. Marker explains, "We feel quite strongly that the ultimate key to the long-term survival of cheetahs lies in our ability to educate people about cheetahs and to show them why it's important to maintain a healthy population of cheetahs. We know that if nothing is done, the cheetah could be gone within 20 years. We cannot let that happen.

"We at CCF are attacking the problems facing cheetahs in their struggle to survive in several ways. One of the strategies employed by CCF that has been quite successful in eliminating the primary cause of conflicts between livestock owners and cheetahs is our Livestock Guarding Dog Program."

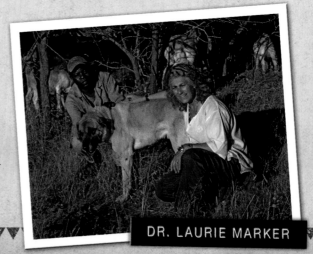

DR. LAURIE MARKER

The Cheetah Conservation Fund, founded by Dr. Laurie Marker (shown here), helps save cheetahs by placing Anatolian shepherd dogs with farmers in Namibia.

Dr. Marker continues, "CCF began placing livestock guarding dogs on farms in Namibia in 1994. Since that time, CCF has placed more than 300 of these dogs, and most farmers who have the dogs reported a 100 percent drop in livestock losses to cheetahs and other predators."

The guard dogs CCF chose for its Livestock Guarding Dog Program are Anatolian shepherd dogs. These dogs are expensive—far too costly for most African farmers to buy. There is a long waiting list of farmers who'd like to have one, but only if there is little or no charge. To help, the Livestock Guarding Dog Program offers some African farmers the dogs at no charge or for a small fee, depending on each farmer's ability to pay for the dogs. This breed was chosen for the program because these dogs are very aggressive about protecting herds. Cheetahs tend to be timid, so they run away when they see and hear these large, barking guard dogs heading for them—and running away means they will live to hunt another day.

Anatolian Shepherd Dogs: Why These Dogs?

Throughout history, people have used dogs to protect their livestock herds from predators. Turkish herders have depended on a particular dog breed to guard their livestock for more than 6,000 years. The breed draws its name from Anatolia, the ancient name for Turkey and its surrounding area. Scientists tell us that Anatolian shepherd dogs can be linked to a breed of large hunting dog that lived in ancient Mesopotamia.

Through the centuries, Anatolian shepherd dogs have been bred specifically to be excellent guard dogs. Certain behaviors have been emphasized by breeders that, over time, have produced dogs with great strength and stamina. These dogs are also quite fearless, which is an essential quality for dogs that are expected to challenge dangerous predators. They can

ANATOLIAN SHEPHERD DOG

Name: Anatolian Shepherd Dog
Type: Mammal
Diet: Carnivore
Average lifespan: 12 to 15 years
Height: 29 to 32 inches (74 to 81 cm) at the shoulder (male)
        27 to 31 inches (68 to 70 cm) at the shoulder (female)
Weight: 110 to 143 pounds (50 to 65 kg) (male)
        88 to 120 pounds (40 to 54 kg) (female)

Most of modern Turkey was known as Anatolia in ancient times.

travel great distances and work in large, open areas as the herds they guard move across the arid Anatolian region of Turkey and Asia Minor. The weather there is very similar to that in Namibia in the southern part of Africa—very little rainfall, extremely hot temperatures in the summer, and cold temperatures in the winter. As a result, Anatolian shepherd dogs are also ideal for guarding livestock in Africa.

Anatolian shepherd dogs are built to endure temperature extremes. They have double coats of medium-length fur that insulate the dogs against the blistering summer sun and the cold winter winds in both Turkey and Africa. Many Anatolian shepherd dogs have dark shading around their faces, known as "masks," that prevent the sun's rays from blinding them when they're on patrol during the day.

As adults, these large and imposing dogs have sturdily built bodies that give any predator reason to think twice before challenging them. They typically have large heads and chests with tapering bodies. Females are a bit smaller, but no less aggressive and fearless. These dogs also have excellent eyesight, keen hearing, protective instincts, and a fearsome bark that is often enough to scare off predators.

Training Guard Dogs

Anatolian shepherd dogs begin their training early. At seven or eight weeks of age, Anatolian puppies are weaned from their mothers and taken to live with the livestock herds they will grow up to protect. Experience has shown that puppies of that age have the most success in bonding with the animals of a herd. Once a puppy has been introduced to the herd, it goes out with the human herder and the livestock to become familiar with the behaviors of the herd animals—and to become aware of the wild animals in the area. Human contact with the young dog is kept to a minimum, so its strongest connection is with the herd animals. Humans still carefully supervise each puppy and make sure it is learning its job as a guard dog.

Anatolian shepherd dogs live with their herds around the clock: eating, sleeping, and traveling with the livestock. Although these guard dogs will encounter a variety of predators—including cheetahs, caracals, jackals, baboons, leopards, and occasionally humans—they are not taught to chase or attack predators. The Anatolian shepherd dog's bark and imposing size are enough to make predators run away.

The effects of the Livestock Guarding Dog Program have been encouraging: Recent CCF's surveys show that farmers in Namibia now have more respect for the endangered wild cats, so fewer cheetahs are being killed. The cheetah population is now stable at around 3,000. The next step is to find ways to keep this and other programs going (and growing), so the cheetah and other endangered animals are safe from extinction.

In Turkey, Anatolian shepherd dogs have been bred for centuries, first by the humble shepherds who used the guard dogs to protect their flocks, and later by breeders. These distinctive dogs didn't arrive in the United States until the 1950s. They are popular with breeders here and in other parts of the world, but a word to the wise: These strong-headed dogs aren't for everyone. Be sure to do plenty of research before getting any new pet.

Kangal Dogs:
Similar but Not the Same

For many centuries, shepherds in Turkey have used another livestock-guarding dog: the Kangal dog. These dogs come from the small town of Kangal, located in a remote area of central Turkey. Because that area has been isolated from the outside world for most of its history, Kangal dogs have not been crossbred with other dogs. As a result, Kangal dogs have kept their original characteristics as a unique dog breed.

Because Kangal dogs and Anatolian shepherd dogs look and behave so much alike, some people refer to Anatolian shepherd dogs as Kangal dogs. However, dog breeders recognize them as distinctly different breeds. Both breeds are outstanding livestock-guarding dogs, so the Cheetah Conservation Fund began to include Kangal dogs in their Livestock Guarding Dog Program in 2008. They have been just as effective as Anatolian shepherd dogs in protecting Namibian livestock herds from cheetahs and other African predators.

KANGAL DOGS

HIDE-N-SEEK

CHASE

Paws and Claws

A young cheetah crouches silently in the grass, his gaze fixed on the unsuspecting puppy frolicking just a few yards away. When the puppy rolls onto its back, wiggling in delight, the cheetah slinks down even more and inches closer and closer.

Suddenly, with the explosive quickness that only a cheetah can call upon when attacking its prey, the young predator bounds forward, and in little more than a heartbeat, pounces on the startled puppy. "Yowl!" the puppy cries out as the cheetah traps it. Then the two animals tumble over and over in a rolling ball of fur and claws.

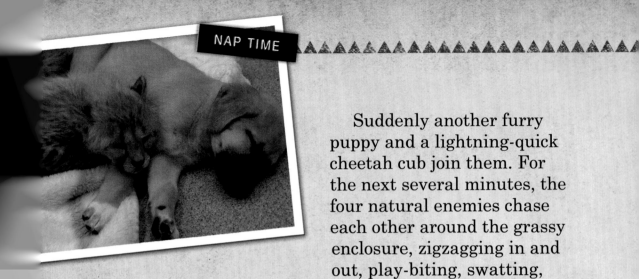

Suddenly another furry puppy and a lightning-quick cheetah cub join them. For the next several minutes, the four natural enemies chase each other around the grassy enclosure, zigzagging in and out, play-biting, swatting, growling, chirping, and wrestling each other. What might seem like a life-and-death struggle among mortal enemies is, in reality, just a playful romp, ending with none of them hurt and all of them ready for a long afternoon nap.

The two cheetah cubs and two Anatolian shepherd puppies are best of friends, and they play together in an exercise yard at the Columbus Zoo and Aquarium in Columbus, Ohio. In the wild, these animals would never live together, so why would a zoo think this is a good idea? The answer is surprising, and it's all about saving cheetahs.

Even as "frenemies" get older, they still enjoy playing together at the zoo.

To clear up this mystery, Jack Hanna, Director Emeritus of the Columbus Zoo and host of *Jack Hanna's Into the Wild* television program, makes it a priority to tell people about what is going on—and what the Columbus Zoo and other concerned groups across the country are doing.

Jack says, "At the Columbus Zoo, we thought we could put pairs of young cheetah cubs and Anatolian shepherd puppies together and raise them to be friends. That would allow us to train them, so they can travel together to television programs, into schools, and to other settings to help us tell the public about how Anatolian shepherd dogs are helping save cheetahs from disappearing. We think that once people understand how important it is to get more of these dogs on more farms in Africa, they'll help us raise the money it takes to do that."

Former Columbus Zoo Director, Jeff Swanagan, cited the importance of this cheetah conservation project as a perfect example of his belief that zoos should "touch the heart to teach the mind." He understood that when people feel strongly about something, like cheetahs disappearing, they become eager learners. People who are made aware of why and how cheetahs are disappearing become strong supporters of projects that focus on saving cheetahs from possible extinction. The zoo's program teaches children and adults how Anatolian shepherd dogs are helping save cheetahs in Africa. Learning more about these livestock-guarding dogs will also help people see that dogs and cheetahs truly can be "frenemies for life."

JEFF SWANAGAN

Sadly, Jeff Swanagan passed away in 2009, but his vision to "touch the heart to teach the mind" continues to guide programs at the Columbus Zoo.

Raising and Training Cubs and Pups

These cubs and puppies have been living together since they were just a few weeks old—almost as if they were litter mates. The Columbus Zoo's involvement in this unique cheetah conservation project began in November 2008, when three baby cheetahs were born at the Cincinnati Zoo. Two males from the litter were chosen by the Columbus Zoo to be included in the project, and the third cub from the litter stayed at the Cincinnati Zoo to be part of a similar project for cheetah conservation there.

Shortly after the cheetah cubs were born, members of the Columbus Zoo's Promotions Department drove to Attalla, Alabama, to pick up two female Anatolian shepherd puppies at the Clear Creek's Anatolian Kennels. The puppies were from an extremely large litter of thirteen puppies—too many for their mom to take care of properly. Because some of the puppies would have to be hand-raised by people anyway, providing them to the Columbus Zoo for its special program turned out to be a good solution for everyone.

From the beginning, the cheetah cubs, Ro and Reh (pronounced "ray"), and the Anatolian puppies, Ruth and Reese, have gotten along very well. They have played together like best friends and have shared their water dishes and cozy rugs for naps since they were first put together.

Naming the Cheetahs

Jack Hanna explains how the cheetah cubs got their unusual names. "We decided that the cheetahs should have African names, so we named one Roho, which means 'spirit' in Swahili, and we named the other one Sherehe, which means 'celebration.' They were given those names in honor of Heather Pick, a television news anchor at WBNS-10TV in Columbus, Ohio. In her lifetime, Heather was an active supporter of the zoo. She loved all types of animals, and she was especially active in promoting wildlife conservation causes. Tragically, Heather passed away from cancer, but her spirit lives on at the zoo, and her concern for wildlife is celebrated in this book and through the zoo's wildlife conservation programs."

HEATHER PICK

Suzi Rapp from the Columbus Zoo helps get Reese, Ruth, Ro, and Reh ready for their appearance on *Good Morning America*.

© Ida Mae Astute/American Broadcasting Company, Inc.

The young cheetah cubs and the Anatolian shepherd puppies are trained every day by the Columbus Zoo Promotions Department staff. According to department head, Suzi Rapp, the training is designed to prepare the cubs and puppies so they won't be anxious or frightened by the sights and sounds they'll encounter in a television studio or at a school with hundreds of kids wiggling around nearby.

"We've raised these guys to not be upset by noises or by people moving around," explains Suzi. "We feel confident that we can take them into any setting, and they'll remain calm and under control at all times. The training these little zoo ambassadors receive is quite similar to the training you might give your dog at home, making sure they correctly respond to the commands they're given no matter what is going on around them."

Meet the Frenemies

Reh

Ro

Reh is very ambitious and loves to explore. He is independent, but he is also a lover and seeks out affection.

Ro is very laid back; nothing seems to bother him. He likes affection but doesn't seek it out.

Reese

Reese is definitely the pack leader. She is confident, and her nature is to protect.

Ruth

Ruth loves affirmation and affection, and has little moments here and there of great confidence.

Animal Ambassadors

Ro, Reh, Reese, and Ruth may not look like important diplomats, but they are—as animal ambassadors for cheetah conservation.

Animal Ambassador programs are a zoo's way of bringing the zoo animals and information to the public. The programs are educational presentations in which zoo staff and/or volunteers take animals out into the community (or onto the zoo grounds) to allow people to see zoo animals "up close and personal." Animal Ambassador programs are an important way for zoos to educate the public about the role of wildlife in the balance of nature and the critically important need to conserve all of our natural resources.

If you've visited a zoo recently, you've probably seen zoo representatives displaying and talking about different animals—from snakes to elephants. They talk about the creature's physical characteristics, behaviors, geographic range, and threatened or endangered status. Some zoos, including the Columbus Zoo, also present "wildlife shows" that feature

animals exhibiting their normal behaviors as zoo staff gives
in-depth information about the animals and their natural
environment. You also may have been lucky enough to have
your local zoo bring some wild animals to visit your school.

For many years, the Columbus Zoo and Aquarium has
had exceptional success taking animals out to meet the
public. "Jungle" Jack Hanna regularly takes animals to
shows and events around the country to promote the zoo
and wildlife conservation. Ro, Reh, Reese, and Ruth have
accompanied Jack to *Good Morning America*, *The Late Show
with David Letterman*, *Larry King Live*, *On the Record with
Greta VanSusteren*, and many other radio and television
programs. When Jack visits those programs, he explains the
important role they're playing in cheetah conservation, and
a huge audience of viewers and listeners learn about the
CCF's Livestock Guarding Dog Program.

Suzi Rapp explains, "The cubs and puppies have even been guests at the White House, where they entertained President Barack Obama's two daughters, Sasha and Malia. But no matter where Animal Ambassadors go, they play a vitally important role in educating the public about wildlife and in helping to raise money for wildlife conservation."

Animal Ambassador programs, like the Columbus Zoo Animal Encounters Program, help fund a wide range of conservations efforts. For example, a portion of the proceeds from each Columbus Zoo Animal Encounters Program event is donated to the zoo's conservation fund. That fund helps support many of the conservation projects being conducted both at the zoo and in many countries around the world—including the CCF so it can purchase Anatolian shepherd dogs to be placed on farms in Africa.

Wildlife conservation is a top priority, not only in Columbus, but also at zoos around the world. Let's take a look at how zoos work together to protect animals and maintain their survival.

Cheetah Conservation:
A Zoo View

Wildlife conservation tops the list of important things zoos do. Many zoos today have full-time staff, and in some cases entire departments, devoted to managing the zoo's various conservation projects. Some of those projects are carried out on the zoo's grounds with animals in the zoo's collection. Other projects are located in the parts of the world where the animals live. Those projects are overseen by zoo staff, by wildlife biologists from conservation organizations, and/or by colleges and universities.

At the Columbus Zoo, Conservation Coordinator Rebecca Rose is the person in charge of conservation programs. She explains the role the Columbus Zoo has played in the conservation of cheetahs and numerous other endangered species from around the world: "The Columbus Zoo has had a long-standing

REBECCA ROSE

A cheetah mother with five cubs in the Masai Mara game reserve in Kenya.

commitment to the conservation of wildlife and wild places. Through our Conservation Grants Program, the zoo provides support to more than seventy projects in thirty countries each year. In only the past five years, the zoo has contributed 3.8 million dollars to protect wildlife around the globe—from the critically endangered freshwater mussels of North America to the cheetahs of southern Africa.

"Cheetah conservation has been a zoo priority since the Fund for Cheetahs was created in 2001 by the Promotions Department. Since then, the zoo has contributed $150,000 to protect cheetahs in Africa. Projects receiving support from the zoo's Fund for Cheetahs include the Cheetah Conservation Fund in Namibia, Action for Cheetahs in Kenya, the Ann van Dyk Cheetah Centre, the Anatolian Shepherd Guard Dog Project in South Africa, and the Matabeleland Leopard and Cheetah Project in Zimbabwe."

In addition to working with organizations like those above, the Columbus Zoo also works with other zoos to promote cheetah conservation.

Zoos Working Together: AZA

Zoos work closely together to give animals like cheetahs a fighting chance of surviving into the future. In 1924, zoos in North America joined together to form an organization that established professional standards for all zoos to work toward. That organization, known today as the Association of Zoos and Aquariums (AZA), is a "nonprofit organization dedicated to the advancement of accredited zoos and aquariums in the areas of animal care, wildlife conservation, education, and science."[1] When a zoo or aquarium reaches the standards set by AZA in all of those areas, AZA puts its stamp of approval on that facility and officially recognizes it as an accredited, or recognized, AZA-member institution.

According to AZA Executive Director, Kristin Vehrs, "One of the most important areas of emphasis for our organization is conservation, and with more than two hundred accredited zoos and aquariums, AZA is developing North America's largest wildlife conservation movement."

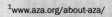

[1]www.aza.org/about-aza/

Ms. Vehrs points out that the investment in the conservation of endangered wildlife species by AZA zoos and aquariums around the globe is extremely impressive: "Over the last five years alone, AZA-accredited institutions have supported 3,693 conservation projects in more than 100 countries with financial assistance in excess of 89 million dollars."

One of the primary ways that AZA and its member institutions work together to prevent the extinction of wildlife species is by developing a game plan to help individual species survive. These plans are called Species Survival Plans (SSPs). Each SSP provides a detailed step-by-step plan of action that includes captive breeding of a species to ensure that healthy populations of those animals are maintained in zoos and aquariums. The ultimate goal of all conservation strategies for endangered animals is to one day return those animals to healthy population levels in their natural habitats. But the first step is to maintain populations in zoos and aquariums so animals that are in danger do not go extinct.

Ms. Vehrs adds, "SSP species are often 'flagship species,' animals that are very popular with the public, such as the giant panda, California condor, and lowland gorilla. Currently, there are more than 115 AZA Species Survival Plan programs, and every one of those is responsible for developing a master plan for managing each species in zoos and aquariums."

The next time you visit an AZA-accredited zoo or aquarium, you can be proud of the fact that some of the money you spend on your visit will be used to help endangered animals.

The cheetah is also one of those flagship species. According to North American Cheetah SSP Coordinator Jack Grisham of the Saint Louis Zoological Park, "Although cheetahs have been kept in captivity for thousands of years, they're hard to breed in zoos and are often the victims of diseases. Scientists who have conducted research to find out why cheetahs don't breed very well tell us that when cheetahs survived the massive extinction that wiped out the saber-toothed cats and many other species between 10,000 and 20,000 years ago, cheetah populations dropped to such low numbers that a 'genetic bottleneck' was created. That simply means that all cheetahs today came from the same closely related ancestors, which results in poor reproductive success and makes them susceptible to diseases. Despite those serious problems, there are now more than 300 cheetahs in the AZA Cheetah SSP program. So, if some disaster were to wipe out cheetah populations in the wild, we could reintroduce cheetahs into their natural habitats from our stock held in zoos."

By developing close working relationships with conservation organizations that are located in the countries where cheetahs are found, the AZA is playing an important role in securing the future of cheetahs in the wild.

Helping Save the Cheetah

As we have already learned, by developing a number of successful conservation strategies for cheetahs in Africa and the Middle East, Cheetah Conservation Fund has had a significant impact on reversing the trend of cheetahs disappearing from their natural habitat. CCF currently operates cheetah conservation projects in Namibia and assists with projects in Kenya, Botswana, Algeria, Iran, South Africa, and Zimbabwe.

Another organization that is hard at work helping cheetahs is located in De Wildt, South Africa. The Ann van Dyk Cheetah Centre, formerly known as the De Wildt Cheetah Trust, was established in 1971 as a captive breeding site for cheetahs. At that time, it was estimated that as few as 700 cheetahs survived in all of South Africa. Since then, the Cheetah Centre has been highly successful in breeding this endangered species. Over the years, more than 800 cheetah cubs have been born at the Cheetah Centre. Even though cheetahs were the primary focus of the Cheetah Centre at the beginning, many other rare and endangered African animals have benefited from its conservation projects, including blue and red duikers,

ANN van DYK CHEETAH CENTRE

brown hyenas, riverine rabbits, servals, suni antelopes, Egyptian vultures, and African wild dogs. Some of these species have not only been successfully bred at the Cheetah Centre, but they have also been successfully reintroduced into their natural habitats, thus helping to repopulate areas from which these animals had disappeared.

The Cheetah Centre also initiated the Wild Cheetah Management Programme (WCMP). Because there are fewer than 1,000 free-ranging cheetahs in all of South Africa today, much remains to be done to ensure that wild cheetahs will survive there. One way that the WCMP is helping wild cheetah populations is by reducing farmer/cheetah conflicts. The Cheetah Centre relocates problem cheetahs away from farms to areas where they will not be a threat to farmers' livestock.

The Cheetah Centre also places great emphasis on environmental education to teach adults and children about cheetahs and the importance of maintaining healthy cheetah populations in South Africa. The Cheetah Centre conducts extensive educational outreach programs into local and out-lying rural communities.

In addition to its breeding and educational programs, the Cheetah Centre plays an important role in conservation biology by conducting research on wildlife diseases and nutrition. The information gathered from those studies is essential in creating a national plan for the conservation of free-ranging cheetahs in South Africa.

How You Can Help

You don't have to be a zoologist or a wild-cat expert to help cheetahs or other wild animals survive. Your local zoo or aquarium probably has a conservation fund where you can make a donation or ask about any volunteer opportunities for someone your age. You can also help zoos, aquariums, and conservation organizations far from home by checking them out online or by writing to ask about their conservation efforts. You can start with the organizations listed below to find out about ways you can help:

AZA Conservation Endowment Fund
Association of Zoos and Aquariums
8403 Colesville Road, Suite 710
Silver Spring, MD 20910-3314
www.aza.org

Cheetah Conservation Fund
2210 Mt. Vernon Avenue, Suite 301
P.O. Box 2496
Alexandria, VA 22301-0496
www.cheetah.org

Columbus Zoo Fund for Cheetahs
The Columbus Zoo and Aquarium
4850 West Powell Road
P.O. Box 400
Powell, Ohio 43065
www.columbuszoo.org

The Ann van Dyk Cheetah Centre
P.O. Box 1756
0216, Hartbeespoort
South Africa
www.dewildt.co.za

Recommended Reading

American Kennel Club. *The Complete Dog Book for Kids*. Howell House, 1996.

Becker, John E., Ph.D. *Wild Cats: Past & Present*. Plain City, Ohio: Darby Creek Publishing, 2008.

Clutton-Brock, Juliet. *Dog (DK Eyewitness Books)*. DK Children, 2004.

Dawydiak, Orysia and David Sims. *Livestock Protection Dogs, Second Edition*. Alpine Publications, 2004.

Hansen, Rosanna. *Caring for Cheetahs*. Honesdale, Pennsylvania: Boyds Mills Press, 2007.

MacMillan, Dianne M. *Cheetahs: Nature Watch*. Minneapolis, Minnesota: Lerner Publishing Group, 2009.

Mehus-Roe, Kristin. *Dogs for Kids: Everything You Need to Know About Dogs*. BowTie Press, 2007.

National Geographic. "Amazing Animals." *National Geographic Kids Almanac 2010*. National Geographic Children's Books, 2009.

Squire, Ann O. *Cheetahs (True Books)*. Scholastic/Children's Press, 2005.

Urbigkit, Cat. *Brave Dogs, Gentle Dogs: How They Guard Sheep*. Honesdale, Pennsylvania: Boyds Mills Press, 2005.

GLOSSARY

accredited: when a person or organization has been given official recognition or approval.

ambassador: a representative of a country or an organization.

Anatolia: the western peninsula of Asia, bounded by the Black, Aegean, and Mediterranean seas, that forms the greater part of Turkey.

bonding: the forming of a close relationship.

coalition: a group of people or animals united for the mutual benefit of all parties.

conservation biology: the scientific study of the effects human beings have on the environment and on the preservation of biological diversity.

diplomat: an individual skilled at dealing tactfully with others.

ecology: the science of studying the relationship of living things with their environments.

flagship species: the most highly recognized or featured species.

fossilize: the process through which organic matter is transformed into mineral substances over long periods of time.

free-ranging: able to roam freely without restrictions; not confined.

genetic bottleneck: the condition that exists when the members of a species are reduced to a few, resulting in the extremely close genetic relationship of all future members of that species.

Mesopotamia: the ancient name for the land adjacent to the Tigris and Euphrates rivers, east of the Mediterranean Sea, and roughly corresponding to modern Iraq, and parts of Syria, Turkey, and Iran. Considered the birthplace of civilization.

migrate: to move from one geographic area to another, usually on a seasonal cycle.

Pliocene period: the period in Earth's history from approximately 5.2 to 1.6 million years ago.

reintroduce: to bring back, or restore, a species to areas from which it has disappeared or has been removed.

Species Survival Plan (SSP): a plan of action with a logical sequence of events necessary to allow a specific plant or animal species to survive into the future.

Swahili: the language of the Bantu people of East Africa.

wean: a process as part of the natural developmental cycle whereby a baby is gradually given other foods in order to replace its dependence on its mother's milk, and thus on its mother.

BIBLIOGRAPHY

INTERVIEWS

Grisham, Jack, Director of Animal Collections, Saint Louis Zoological Park, and American Zoological Association (AZA) North American Cheetah SSP Coordinator.

Hanna, Jack, Director Emeritus, Columbus Zoo and Aquarium.

Marker, Dr. Laurie, Founder and Executive Director, Cheetah Conservation Fund.

Rapp, Suzi, Director of Promotions, Outreach, and Animal Encounters, Columbus Zoo and Aquarium.

Rose, Rebecca, Field Conservation Coordinator, Columbus Zoo and Aquarium.

Swanagan, Jeff, Executive Director, Columbus Zoo and Aquarium.

Vehrs, Kris, J.D., Executive Director, American Zoological Association (AZA).

ARTICLES

Daily Mail Reporter. "Meet the dog that thinks there's nothing sweetah than a cheetah." *Mail Online*. June 20, 2008.

Netting, Jessa Forte. "Cat Woman's Fast Company." *Discover Magazine*. March, 2005.

BOOKS

Aaseng, Nathan. *The Cheetah*. San Diego, California: Lucent Books, Inc., 2000.

American Kennel Club. *The Complete Dog Book*. New York: Ballantine Books, 2006.

Caro, T.M.. *Cheetahs of the Serengeti Plains*. Chicago: The University Of Chicago Press, 1994.

Denis-Huot, Christine and Michel. *The Lords of the Savannah Leopards & Cheetahs*. Vercelli, Italy: White Star Publishers, 2006.

Kitchner, Andrew. *The Natural History of Wild Cats*. Ithaca, New York: Comstock Publishing Associates, 1991.

Larkin, Dr. Peter and Mike Stockman. *The Ultimate Encyclopedia of Dogs, Dog Breeds, & Dog Care*. London: Southwater, 2005.

Line, Les, ed. *The Audubon Society Book of Wild Cats*. New York: Harry N. Abrams, Inc., 1985.

Schlaepfer, Gloria. *Animal Ways: Cheetahs*. New York: Benchmark Books, 2002.

Scott, Jonathan and Angela. *BBC Big Cat Diary: Cheetah*. London: Collins, 2005.

Seidensticker, Dr. John and Dr. Susan Lumpkin, eds. *Great Cats*. Emmaus, Pennsylvania: Rodale Press, 1991.

Seidensticker, Dr. John and Dr. Susan Lumpkin. *Smithsonian Answer Book—Cats*. Washington, D.C.: Smithsonian Books, 2004.

Simon, Seymour. *Big Cats*. New York: HarperCollins Publishers, 1994.

Continued on next page . . .

. . . Continued from previous page

Sleeper, Barbara. *Wild Cats of the World*. New York: Crown Publishers, Inc., 1995.

Stonehouse, Bernard. *A Visual Introduction to Wild Cats (Animal Watch)*. New York: Checkmark Books, 1999.

Sunquist, Mel and Fiona Sunduist. *Wild Cats of the World*. Chicago: The University of Chicago Press, 2002.

Turner, Alan. *The Big Cats and Their Fossil Relatives*. New York: Columbia University Press, 1997.

Veron, Geraldine. *On The Trail of Big Cats*. Hauppauge, New York: Barron's Nature Travel Guides, 1998.

Weisbord, Merrily and Kim Kachanofe, D.V.M. *Dogs With Jobs Working Dogs Around The World*. New York: Pocket Books, 2000.

Wexo, John Bonnett. *Big Cats (Zoobooks Series)*, Poway, California: Wildlife Education, Ltd., 2003.

Wolf, Joseph. *The Natural History Museum Library: Big Cats*, U.S.A.: Mallard Press, 1992.

Photo Credits: